This book is a work of fiction. Names, characters, places, and incidents either are products of the author's imagination or are used fictitiously. Any resemblance to actual events or locales or persons, living or dead, is entirely coincidental.

The Precious Jewels Monologue

By: Stacey Barlow

Cover Illustrated by Darlene Higgins

Created by Jazzy Kitty Publishing

Logo Designs by Andre M. Saunders/Leroy Grayson

Editor: Anelda L. Attaway

© 2017 Stacey Barlow

ISBN 978-0-9988433-5-3

Library of Congress Control Number: 2017942288

All rights reserved. This book is protected by the copyright laws of the United States of America. This book may not be copied or reprinted for commercial gain or profit. The use of short quotations or occasional page copying for personal or group study is permitted and encouraged. Permission will be granted upon request. For Worldwide Distribution. Printed in the United States of America. Published by Jazzy Kitty Publishing utilizing Microsoft Publishing Software and Bookcover Pro. The Holy Scriptures are from the Holy Bible.

GOD'S DEDICATION

To You Heavenly Father who passeth all understanding. You have continued to give me strength throughout my trials that come upon me. Every day is a different day, but a new day that You have given me to right the wrongs in my life. I know that I am not perfect, but You keep on blessing me. I can't say enough to show my gratitude, my appreciation and my love for You because You are the main One who looked after me and made sure that I was not in harm's way. I thank You for giving me this gift to spread across the world and the talent to take it well beyond my means. Because of You Father, I am here where You need me to be.

Even though I do have my bad days where I'm not at my best, You keep Your angels around to protect me. Thank You for Your Son, Jesus, whom you let carry all our sins to the cross so that we might be saved. There is so much to be thankful for that I can't name them all but, You know my heart. I've learned that in life there is only ONE who will be by my side forever more. Father, You know the desires of my heart and in You, I will put my trust. Thank You for letting me be one of the apples of Your eye. I truly Love and Adore You!

ACKNOWLEDGMENTS

To all the ladies and little girls growing up to become women. Empower yourselves to be the best you can be. Women, be the example that the young girls need you to be--having strength and courage to hold their head up high and say, "I survived this."

To my loving grandmother, Sarah L. Lomax Henderson for giving me a few names for my characters to come alive.

To the sunshine, my only sunshine, my niece, KiAna Smith, for giving me the character JaNee`.

And a very special thanks to all the women in my family living and resting in love. You are my Precious Jewels angels.

To my spiritual sister, Pam Osbey for inspiring me to focus on my writing so that everything else would fall into place, and to my Puerto Rican sister, Anabelle Munoz across the waters who helped me to translate a few things. Thank you so very much.

Special thanks to Darlene Higgins for the outstanding illustration on the book cover.

To my publisher for her undying dedication in making my writing come to life. I really appreciate it.

Titus 2:3-4 The aged women likewise, that they may be in behavior, as becometh holiness, not false accusers, not given to much wine, teachers of good things. That they may teach the young women to be sober, to love their husbands, to love their children.

Praises For Precious Jewels

"This book represents the voice of today's young women" ~Jeff Rivera, Bestselling Author of FOREVER MY LADY

DEDICATIONS

To All the Jewels in the World

~

You Know Who You Are

TABLE OF CONTENTS

INTRODUCTION	i
CHAPTER 1 - Latrice	01
CHAPTER 2 - DaNisha	03
CHAPTER 3 - Felicity	06
CHAPTER 4 - Maria	11
CHAPTER 5 - Samantha	16
CHAPTER 6 - Cornelius	25
CHAPTER 7 - Ayanna	32
CHAPTER 8 - Jenny	36
CHAPTER 9 - Tina	42
CHAPTER 10 - Sasha	47
CHAPTER 11 - Jasmine	52
CHAPTER 12 - Stacie	56
SECTION II - Canvas on Precious Jewels	59
POEM - Canvas	60
CHAPTER 13 - Peter	64
CHAPTER 14 - Mecca	69
CHAPTER 15 - Cobra	75
CHAPTER 16 - Rowan	78

CHAPTER 17 - Chae Ann 82

CHAPTER 18 - DeWayne 87

CHAPTER 19 - JaNee` 91

ABOUT THE AUTHOR 97

INTRODUCTION
Are You Ready to be Exposed?

In the beginning, the Earth was without form or void and darkness was upon the face of the deep. And the Spirit of God moved upon the face of the waters.

On the sixth day, God made man and named him Adam, but did not breathe life into his nostrils until the seventh day. Adam needed a help meet so, God caused a deep sleep to fall upon Adam, and He took one of his ribs, closed up the flesh, made a woman and brought her to Adam. Because God had taken the rib, Adam states bone of my bone, flesh of my flesh, she shall be called WOMAN. Therefore, a man shall leave his father and mother and cleave unto his wife, for they are to be one flesh. The couple was NAKED and not ashamed. It wasn't until after the eating of the tree, the knowledge of the two being naked, the woman was given a name.

Everyone, fictional or real life, has a story to tell. It would be up to them whether they want to tell you the whole truth and nothing but the truth or tell half of the truth. When they tell it, would you believe their story?

It has been said that a person has over 200 personalities {not schizophrenia} but, a way to hide your certain selves when you don't want anyone to know the "true you." At the end of the day, no matter what your decision will be, you are still a Precious Jewel and have Precious Jewels that need to be honored and respected. Respect yourself!

CHAPTER 1

Latrice

I uncrossed my legs for this man that I trusted. In all my days, I would have never thought that this man, the man that I so admire would have done what he did. My family didn't, wouldn't or couldn't believe me. Why would they believe a five-year-old anyway? I'm grown now, but I dealt with those demons all by myself. And the funny part about it was that these demons kept coming back but in different forms. Some didn't leave as the first demon that came into my life, but that was bad enough. How can you fight a 250-pound man smothering you? Easy. Do what he tells you to do and when you get to his most precious area, squeeze as hard as you can so that he can't use it. When you do, watch the funny expression on his face and be sure to duck because, with a reaction like that, they are liable to strike out at you. Never trust a wolf in sheep's clothing. How can you tell? Look into their eyes. You can't run away from the problem. The best thing to do is face them head on and declare, "I refuse to be a victim of circumstance."

I learned that lesson late in life and it cost me a set of twins, my uterus taken out, and self-esteem that has hit rock bottom.

Oh! You wanna know about the twins? Okay, I was with this man who I thought was cool. We kicked it, loved it, and rolled in it until one day he decided that he wanted to use my face as a punching bag. Five months pregnant with his children, he pushed me down a flight of stairs just because he had a bad day. Someone had to rush me to the hospital because he was too stubborn to do it. He left me lying there hemorrhaging. I was bent over in pain. But by the time I got to the hospital, I had miscarried. Later, I found out that he thought the children weren't his. He is now spending life in prison without parole. This gives him some time to think about his actions.

Grade A sanctified and born again and those demons are still chasing me. No one said that it would be easy. And since my mother died, I feel so lost at times because she was my backbone and it seems that I turn to the unusual of persons. Then I realized, it would be too late; they would have used me up to the point where I feel like I have no more love left to give. But for some reason, there seems to be strength pulled out of nowhere and I receive more love to give it back. But only to the one who deserves it. So, I sit still and wait.

CHAPTER 2

DaNisha

I used to ride my bicycle down to the graveyard to visit my great aunt's grave. It has been five years since she has been gone, and I used to tell her everything that was going on in my life.

On this day that I went to the graveyard, there was this man that I had always heard about but I didn't believe in the folktales people talked about. I finally saw him with my own two eyes. He wasn't a bum or anything like that. He was well dressed and well versed. Yes, I conversed with him. I was curious to why people talked about him the way they did. He had this look in his eyes as if he wanted to belong someplace...somewhere. His company interrupted my time with my great aunt, and I was a bit upset about it, but he seemed so very nice.

I didn't tell anyone of the encounter I had with this man because I had promised to stay away from the graveyard just because of him. After the first initial meeting, I couldn't stay away. So, I found myself going back to that same spot where we met that first day. It had gotten to the point where he was bringing food to have a picnic with me. I started looking forward to my outings just to see him. I still remember his breath on my skin. It smelled of beer and peppermint which in my mind smelled sweet. Father would always want to know why I would come home not being hungry. He thought I was sick because I didn't eat at home.

One foggy morning, I set off on my bicycle to meet him. There he was waiting for me with my favorite piece of candy and a huge picnic basket. I never stop to think about where he got the food from. All I knew was that the food that was prepared was delicious. Next thing I knew, I'm waking up with him standing over me with what looked like he was zipping up his pants.

"Oh God, what just happened?" I wasn't thinking clearly, and still not realizing what just occurred. To my surprise, I wasn't dirty. I asked him what happened? He looked at me, smiled and stated that I simply fell asleep, but when I questioned about seeing him standing over me zipping up his pants, his response was just that it was my imagination. I went on believing that. He carried on like nothing went on.

Weeks went by and I was having these dreams of my great aunt and she was trying to tell me something and as stubborn as she was, my father always said that I had taken after her. I never got my visitor when it was time for it, but my father knew what was going on. He couldn't get angry with me because he loved me just that much and I was his only child. So, one day I took my usual bicycle ride to the graveyard to tell the young man I met weeks earlier the news that he was going to be a father.

As I approached the rock he was sitting on, I noticed something extremely bizarre. He was surrounded by glass and torn clothes. I slowly walked up to him and put my hand on his shoulder. He turned to look at me with bloodshot eyes and replied, "I know." He grabbed me by the hand and asked me to pray with him. Not knowing what was going on in his mind, I obliged him in his request because I knew then he needed prayer just as much as I did. Whatever prayer that was prayed, knocked me to the ground. I woke up, and lying next to me was the man's dead body. I guess he couldn't handle the reality of being a father. I found out later how sick this man really was. . .

His name was Legion.

CHAPTER 3

Felicity

All my life I tried to be good, but ever since I was little I was labeled as a liar. I hate labels. I was one of those rebellious kids who didn't care about what other people said about me. I loved me. Naw, I wasn't born with a silver spoon in my mouth, but I made my own way and got what I wanted my way. Okay, yeah you can call me a nerd if you want to, I made the grade and damn proud of it. Throughout my life, I've had girlfriends and boyfriends; more boyfriends than girlfriends. Granted, you must admit that women are as fine as Hell, no matter what size. I just wanted to get in it, feel it, wet it up and pull out, but they never really satisfied me the way I could satisfy myself. Okay, so you may be wondering what kind of sick perverted person am I? A smart one.

I don't do drugs, I don't smoke weed, and I don't drink. I do have a fault though--I'm a sex addict. It started when I was about 12. I tried all the drinks, smokes, and drugs that you could name, but that just didn't get me to the actual high that I wanted.

One night, I was out with one of my honeys and we went to

this club and I was amazed at all the beautiful made up people onstage. I approached the manager of the club to see what I could do to work there. He simply looked at me, licked his lips, smiled and said for me to come to his office. Like a puppy, I followed. I filled out this form and was videotaped for the office records, and probably for the boss' enjoyment. I didn't care at all though. He told me to come back the next night if I was serious.

I went back the next night punctual as my momma always taught me to be. I was there with a huge grin on my face. The boss liked the fact that I was so enthusiastic about what was about to happen. Was I scared? Hell no! To be up onstage was the least of my worries. I was just wanting to see what it was going to be like. I was having fun performing in front of an audience with people who didn't know me or those who came in that knew me, didn't recognize me.

Then I heard, "We are bringing you someone new tonight, so put your hands together and welcome tonight Felicity."

That whole night I had that adrenaline rush everyone always spoke about being onstage. I was so good with the crowd that my boss put me as headliner three nights a week. I was his goldmine in and out of makeup.

I was pulling in $750 the three nights that I was working. No one could do it better than me and when I went home, I went home with extra cash in my pocket and a bouquet of flowers from men who wanted me. Sound crazy? Not to me because I was getting bills paid, and dropping a few heads to a couple of my family members. I didn't tell them where I was getting the money from and I think that they really didn't care since I was taking care of me and my business. On the nights that I wasn't working, I took my girls and guys out to the best restaurants, and when I was feeling real generous, I'd pack a bag and take two of my closest babes on a trip. I look good and I feel good. . .well, at least that's what I have been told by women and not just men.

I enjoyed being onstage, doing my thing and getting paid. Then my boss decided that I needed to work five days out of the seven that were there. Oh man! I'm really living my dream now. I didn't realize his reason for putting me on the way he did. I was the only one pulling in the cash and he needed to make the money to keep the business open.

After work one night, he approached me and asked me for my help. Me still being eager about having the job which I loved, he showed me his account books. As I looked over the books, I realized why he was all screwed up with the business. His numbers were wrong.

He propositioned me with a new position along with the one that I currently had. I took on the challenge of keeping the books on the nights that I didn't have to perform. I really was living the high life then. The late nights staying up in the office was draining me, but I was enjoying the money that I was getting. So, to speak, I was pimpin' the game or the game was pimpin' me. The boss wanted me to stay after work so that he could get his hands on me. He even asked me to get plastic surgery to enhance my looks. I thought about that long and hard. I mean, come on! Someone else to pay for something that's so expensive. I thought I looked damned good. Months went by and I was still doing my thing and not getting tired not one bit. I had a nice spacious home, the quiet time that I need to meditate on my life, but yet, I was selling myself short by doing something that was against all the rules of my upbringing.

I was already in skin deep with this job and with the boss now offering to pay for surgery that I didn't think I needed. Each night I performed after work did the books. I even took the books home because the boss trusted me with them. Oh yeah, I was excellent in math in college and accounting came easily to me. My boss didn't tell me about his plans. I mean, why would he? I'm just an employee.

I got a call one morning to meet with my boss' lawyer. What the Hell?! Why am I being called in to see my boss' lawyer? Okay, don't panic, it might just be some legal tenders that need to be taken care of. I got to the lawyer's office to find that my boss had recently passed and put me in his will. He was so intrigued by me that he willed his business over to me; stocks, bonds and the extra money he saved with the surprise of taking me on a trip to Jamaica. In my mind, I wonder why would he have wanted to take me there? I'm not family or a spouse. Not that I couldn't be that to him anyway. That would let more skeletons out of his closet that he would have ever wanted. I'm glad that I received things the right way without having to be conniving about things. Even though my life wasn't right to my family the way they envisioned it to be, but it was perfect for me.

I am a former drag queen and the owner of Labels, and my name is Felicity.

CHAPTER 4

Maria

Things like this were not supposed to happen in my family. Not my family, and for many years this "thing" went on behind closed doors and I cried every night because I wanted so desperately to tell someone, ANY one. All I ever heard was "*Callete, No digamos*" What was with him anyway? Couldn't he find a lady to love him enough? The answer was "no" because he was too busy poking me and getting his rocks off every time he felt like he was frustrated. I looked up to Jose` because he was the only one in the family in whom I could trust. I went to him with everything until the night he decided to climb into my bedroom window after curfew thinking that staying in my room would make a difference. He still was going to get in trouble by morning.

At first, I thought he might have mistaken me for one of those females he had taken out that night, but obviously, he knew where he was.

"*Que estas haciendo?*" I'd ask him, but he would tell me the same old thing, "*Callete, No digamos.*"

I always said the same thing; that I would tell. He wouldn't let up, my own brother wouldn't stop, couldn't stop. All I know is that he needed help, and in my eyes, I will always love him, but only the way a sister should.

At first, it was innocent. I know, how can you say something like that was innocent? But it was. He climbed into my bed and I really didn't think about it because he'd always come to my room, climb under the covers, and lie close to me, holding me. So, to me, it was natural for him to do that but, it went too far this time. Why was he doing this to his own sister? No one knows really but him.

It was August, the month our younger hermano died. Jose` claimed that I was the only one who understood the pain he felt when little Edwardo died. It was an accident and Jose` blamed himself for it. Maybe that was just an excuse to climb into my bed at night. He used that sorrowful excuse for what seemed like an eternity to me because when he touched me, he seemed angry at me and at the world. There was no other excuse than just him missing his brother. Like I didn't miss my brother too, but, I didn't use that as an excuse to get off on anybody.

I just knew that if I didn't do anything, I would be scarred for life. My psyche couldn't handle that, and to be honest, I believe Jose` couldn't either. I walked around like a zombie most days. My grades started to slip and I was called into the principal's office more times than a little within a two-month period. That is not good on my record when my parents knew that I was a straight "A" student. How I managed to keep that straight "A" average was a blessing. I then started acting out just because I thought I could get away with it. I had boys falling to my feet wanting to be with me, but no one could treat me better than my brother would. I became use to my brother coming into my room at night. It started to feel natural as if I belonged to him and he belonged to me. Strange really.

I was mad as Hell at him for taking my virginity. That sounds funny huh? "Mad as Hell" First of all, dogs get mad, I am a female, and secondly Hell would be hot, right? We really should change the way we say things. Jose` was my everything. It was just me and him against the world. There was nothing we couldn't do. Even when papi would come home from a hard day's work, and want to throw a fit because something in the house wasn't done to his liking, Jose` would have my back when papi tried to come at me. I had Jose's back when papi raised his fist at him. I learned how to fight in that household but, why didn't I fight back when it came to Jose`? I don't really know.

It was Christmas Eve and I had to work that night at Bogos.

The Precious Jewels Monologue

We had pulled a doubled shift, and I needed the money for the holidays. Papi couldn't say that I wasn't pulling my weight because I had a decent job, or so I thought. I like the job. It gave me the freedom to move around and I was in line for a promotion. I remember going into work that night but, by the second shift, I was nearly out of it. I had received a call earlier from Jose` telling me that he had a surprise for me when I got home. I was all excited about whatever it was he had waiting for me at home.

12 o'clock came around and it was time for me to clock out. I couldn't get out of there quick enough. It seemed to take longer to get home from work than it did to get to work. It was cold so, I had bundled up real tight, and took two trains and a cab to get home. It was Christmas morning technically, so I was all ready to get my surprise. I handed the cab driver $10 and told him to keep the change. Knowing really, I couldn't afford to give him a tip, but I was in a generous mood. I said goodnight and close the cab door and ran up the steps to my house. Still excited about the call that I received earlier from Jose`.

I put the key in the keyhole and took a deep breath. There was no sound in the house whatsoever. I called out to papi and

Jose` a few times. As I walked into the dining room, I noticed the table set for three and the sweet smell of Pollo was done and ready to eat. I called again for papi and Jose`. There was still no answer. I walked down the hall, taking off the rest of the warm clothing I had on. As I was pulling off my glove, I noticed a dim light in the den. I walked slowly into the room where our favorite singer was rotating on the stereo, Celia Cruz and for some reason, the record was skipping. That had never happened before. As I went over to the stereo to turn it off, out the corner of my eye I saw a hand. I moved a little closer to see what or who it was. There on the cold wooden floor lied Jose`. I leaned over to what I thought was his dead body, he reached up and grabbed my hand and whispered, "Papi knows." and with his last breath, Jose` said, "Te Amo." Papi was nowhere to be found.

CHAPTER 5

Samantha

My momma told me that there would be days like this. I thought she was lying about those coming of days. As a little girl growing up, my momma taught me many things about my body. From keeping my hair, nails, and skin tight to the sophistication of a walk when I'm out. I really wasn't being bothered by the "boys" at school because I was all about my grades. My momma also taught me the importance of a good education too. Now, I'm not saying that I'm all that and a bad bag of Oreo cookies, I'm just saying that I am the best and men need that in their lives.

I caught the attention of an executive as I was walking down Nectar Street one afternoon. This man was hella fine to be White. He was the splitting image of Joshua Morrow, the actor from "The Young and The Restless." I swear that man could have been his twin brother. He had this kind of swagger about him that could make ducks fall from the sky. He was just that fine. So, anyway, he stopped me in the middle of the street on the crosswalk of course and told me how beautiful I was. At first, I was flattered--then I thought, *"Hey now, why is he stopping me in the middle of the walkway just to tell me something that I already know?"* I smiled and said thank you as I proceeded to tell him in my well-behaved manner that he didn't look so bad himself knowing all the while I really wanted to jump his bones.

Pump your breaks sistah and listen to your head. My detectors went off and I scoped this guy out. Hmmm, no wedding ring or wedding ring print. Okaaaay, he must have babies somewhere.

My mind snapped back in to reality and I focused on those gorgeous lips which just told me how beautiful I was. He licked them once, twice and the third time, then I remembered this man is talking to me and I didn't get his name. Without me even asking, he said his name was Bryce, Bryce Stillmore. He owned a computer software company on the west side. I didn't take his card when he handed it to me because there was a caution going around stating that this was a new wave of men stealing by some type of chemical being on the card that makes the victim sick. Instead, I put his number in my Lotus. I didn't want to tell him where I worked because it was just something that I could do while I found a better position but, I told him anyway after he asked. It turns out that I worked at Labels a few blocks from his company. He offered to drop by and see me

CHAPTER 5

Samantha

My momma told me that there would be days like this. I thought she was lying about those coming of days. As a little girl growing up, my momma taught me many things about my body. From keeping my hair, nails, and skin tight to the sophistication of a walk when I'm out. I really wasn't being bothered by the "boys" at school because I was all about my grades. My momma also taught me the importance of a good education too. Now, I'm not saying that I'm all that and a bad bag of Oreo cookies, I'm just saying that I am the best and men need that in their lives.

I caught the attention of an executive as I was walking down Nectar Street one afternoon. This man was hella fine to be White. He was the splitting image of Joshua Morrow, the actor from "The Young and The Restless." I swear that man could have been his twin brother. He had this kind of swagger about him that could make ducks fall from the sky. He was just that fine. So, anyway, he stopped me in the middle of the street on the crosswalk of course and told me how beautiful I was. At first, I was flattered--then I thought, *"Hey now, why is he stopping me in the middle of the walkway just to tell me something that I already know?"* I smiled and said thank you as I proceeded to tell him in my well-behaved manner that he didn't look so bad himself knowing all the while I really wanted to jump his bones.

Pump your breaks sistah and listen to your head. My detectors went off and I scoped this guy out. Hmmm, no wedding ring or wedding ring print. Okaaaay, he must have babies somewhere.

My mind snapped back in to reality and I focused on those gorgeous lips which just told me how beautiful I was. He licked them once, twice and the third time, then I remembered this man is talking to me and I didn't get his name. Without me even asking, he said his name was Bryce, Bryce Stillmore. He owned a computer software company on the west side. I didn't take his card when he handed it to me because there was a caution going around stating that this was a new wave of men stealing by some type of chemical being on the card that makes the victim sick. Instead, I put his number in my Lotus. I didn't want to tell him where I worked because it was just something that I could do while I found a better position but, I told him anyway after he asked. It turns out that I worked at Labels a few blocks from his company. He offered to drop by and see me sometime and offered to pick me up after work. Did I really want him coming there seeing he seemed to be an outstanding gentleman? Sure, why not?

I was off and he wasn't doing anything at that moment so we went for brunch. Okay, so the guy owns his own company, but I wasn't thinking that this guy was extremely loaded. He didn't come off as the type that had a lot of money. I was just thinking how interesting it was to own his own company. So why didn't I think that way about Felicity? Because she acquired that business, Bryce started from the bottom up with his. He didn't give me that sob story about growing up hard, that his parents were divorced or that he had a rough childhood. He seemed to be into what was going on with me; my goals and dreams, and where I'd like to be in five years. Why just five though, why not 10? That number would give me a better outlook on where I'd like to be without rushing things.

As he concentrated on what I had to say about where I wanted to be in five years, I could see that brain working in his head planning his next move. Being as smart as I am and remembering what my momma taught me, I stopped in mid-sentence and told him I was more interested in what was on his mind. That was a loaded question because I already knew what was on his mind. I let time slip away from me because I was enjoying Bryce's company but, I had some other errands to run. He was being a gentleman until the very end of the brunch we just had. Since we exchanged numbers earlier on and seeing that he was a very busy individual, I declined his offer to take me where I needed to go. I told him maybe next time. We ended that day on a lovely note and I wondered how many other women did he swoon that way? Oh well, he was just a man on the street who I had brunch with.

Felicity called me into work because she ended up being shorthanded. I was happy to oblige her because I needed the money. Bryce called me around 10 o'clock that night and left me a message because I was still at work.

On my break, I checked my calls and received a message that Bryce was coming to my job to see me. I went about my usual routine as if the call didn't exist. Fifteen til 11, in walked Bryce, dressed down but still looking good. Obviously, he's not new to the spot because everyone there seemed to know him. Felicity pointed him in my direction. I walked up to him casually to greet him and there he pulled out one single yellow rose.

"I stopped by to just say hello, not going to stay long. I will call you in two days." And that he did.

I had to be some kind of special to this guy because, for the next three dates, he pulled out all the stops, taking me to the most expensive restaurants, shutting down department stores to take me shopping, romantic carriage rides in the park at night, and flowers at my door. The fourth date was a test of how far I wanted to go with this man. Yes, my momma knew about him.

"Baby just as long as he is nice to you and the heart is right, be happy."

The fourth date was at his place. Had that rich kind of food. You know the kind that a woman like me can only dream about? Yeah, that kind.

As the night progressed with jazz music and a starlit night, we walked out onto the balcony to look over the city. As I said, it was that kind of fantasy that only girls like me dream of. He asked me what was on my mind, and I couldn't really explain to him the feeling that I received being that high up. Not that I was trying to be materialistic or anything. The view from up there was breathtaking. The night air was blowing just right and I was feeling the jazz Bryce was playing in the background.

Bryce eased up behind me and whispered in my ear, "What if I wanted to take you away from all this? I mean away from your job to come work for me getting paid triple the amount that you're getting paid now?"

What the man didn't realize was that I loved what I was doing. Besides, it's our fourth date and I felt we didn't know each other that well, but in reality, we did or at least we were going to get to know each other that night. He cupped my face with his hands, looked deep into my eyes and told me how beautiful I was. I couldn't believe what this man was telling me. It all sounded unreal so, with each word he said to me, I asked him to repeat it. He had this giggle and smile about him. He wasn't ashamed to tell me again without getting angry. He said it again. . .we had the kind of night where morning came too soon. Feeling like an angel on clouds, even the bed was amazing.

I woke to the smell of breakfast being brought to the room. On the breakfast tray was a note and a yellow rose saying that Bryce had an emergency meeting that he had to attend and he'd be back as soon as he could. Being the lady that I am, I couldn't stay. I had errands to run again today. Since he was in a meeting, I left him a note telling him that I had to run errands that day and check on my momma. I was hoping to run into him on the street, but for some reason, the streets were crowded.

I went to check on momma to see how she was feeling and decided that we could have a ladies day out.

We started with brunch since it was midafternoon. As we settled into the lovely bistro, momma asked me how I was doing with Bryce since she hadn't seen much of me. She had this grin on her face and I was wondering why she was smiling the way she was. Bryce was standing behind me with another yellow rose. Loving the way, he did things, he didn't stay long and stated that he'd see me later that night.

Six months passed and Bryce was still doing those romantic things he did when he first met me. He propositioned me again about working with him at his company.

"I'll say it again, I love what I do at Labels."

He gave me some time to think about it, and I agreed with a stipulation that I could work on the weekends at Labels. Bryce hesitated a second or two, looked deep into my eyes and said, "Sure, as long as you give your two weeks notice to Felicity."

The night was filled with magic, food, jazz, and love or, so I thought.

Bryce moved me and my momma into his condo. Momma was moved into the guest house where she could move around freely. She was close so that I could keep an eye on her. I could spend more time with her when I had that kind of time since I was now working with Bryce.

Each Wednesday we all went out on the town. I never really understood the reason for the Wednesday night outings but, I never complained about it at all. I was having the time of my life.

Thursday night was strangely different. Momma wasn't home. I found out that Bryce sent her out on the town with a few of momma's friends so that he and I could have our time alone. I never wonder what he's up to because he is always on the up and up. As usual, we had our romantic dinner out. We came home and once there, my eyes deceived me with the array of yellow roses placed here and there in the house. The rose petals led to the balcony.

Bryce escorted me to the balcony all the while enjoying an enlightening conversation. Not thinking he was going to do anything. There was candlelight, more yellow roses, and dessert. He knew I loved cheesecake so, I knew then something had to be up. He fed me every bite of that cheesecake and with every bite that I took, there was a kiss to follow. It was just a slice or two, and both were finished. Weird combination of champagne and cheesecake. . .you would think he'd have a

The Precious Jewels Monologue

glass of milk with that. I just got used to what was given to me.

Bryce took a deep breath and pulled out a box.

"Oh no! Not the box."

I calmed my nerves because it could have been a pair of earrings, right? He got down on one knee and opened the box. Sitting high inside that box was a 3.5-carat marquis canary yellow diamond ring.

"Samantha, the love of my life, will you do me the honor of being my wife?"

With no hesitation, I said, "Yes!"

And the night was filled with more jazz, magic, and love or, so I thought. And to my surprise, I finally found out what Bryce was all about. I couldn't very well take back my answer. Don't get me wrong, I had fallen in love with this man and I loved him because we had fun together.

I'm sure he loved me in his own little way, but for the most part, he put it another way.

"Relax, it's just sex."

CHAPTER 6

Cornelius

Every woman wanted me, but I didn't want every woman. I'm not saying that I went around screwing every woman that walked by me and got me to stand at attention. Most men have certain things they look for in a woman. I'm a different kind of species. I'm not the one who like those ghetto fabulous chicks or gold diggers. I can spot them a mile away. I'm not the best-looking brother, but hey I get by. I knew the women used me for whatever purpose they needed, and for some stupid reason, I didn't mind, right? Wrong. I want a woman who can give me "her" spiritually, mentally and emotionally. Don't get it twisted, I told you I was different.

Every relationship will have something in it to make it go sour, and the person left hurt has to caution him or herself of the next person who comes along. I'm not out to hurt anybody because I don't want to be hurt. I've had three relationships. I have to admit, I made some stupid mistakes in the past with these young ladies, and they didn't deserve to be treated that way. I'm not going to go into any details about what happened to them because that would take forever the way I tell my story.

The Precious Jewels Monologue

But I will tell you this, I was viewed as a "Dog" to some just because I'm known around town.

There is this one fine ass woman that I've been trying to holla at for what seemed like a hell of a long time. I mean, Femme Fatale had it going on to me, and sister had me working hard to get with her and make her believe that I was the real deal. I'm not saying that she was playing hard to get; the girl was damaged. She had been through so many relationships throughout her life that this last fellow just did it in for her.

When I met her, Femme was all smiles and things because someone paid her some attention. Not me, the other cat that messed up her mind. She really wasn't trying to talk to me when I saw her, but I knew that I'd see her again.

I had a chance when I saw her one day and she wasn't smiling. I'm surprised that she remembered me. I asked her why was she looking all sad? That it couldn't be that bad whatever it was that was going on. She gave me a half-hearted smile. I asked her if I could join her, but that I didn't want to impose. She gestured for me to take a seat.

As I was trying to rap to this sister, my phone kept going off. She was probably thinking that I was a pimp by how much my phone was going off. But honestly, she really didn't have to worry about me not paying attention to her. I got her comfortable enough to tell me what was really going on with her.

This other cat, Mo got baby girl's nose wide open, but brother claiming he's confused about how he feels about her. This dude is out of his mind if he can't see that he has a diamond on his hand. I'm not one to dog another brother about what he has, but it sounds to me like this brother doesn't want her. So, then if he doesn't want her, why is he messing with her mind like that? I was going to see if she would let me try to put that smile back on her face. I offered a movie and a free concert on Nectar Street. Prince was playing over there in Cinnamon Garden on the main. I told her free, but I was willing to pay for that trip.

I wondered if she had to call old boy to let him know that she was going out with a friend, but to my surprise, she didn't call him. I guess she decided that she needed to do something different for a change. I wanted to get her mind off him and I think I succeeded. I didn't see no ring on her finger, and she did tell me that old boy said that she didn't belong to him. Playbook rule time! I intercepted old dude's ball and I'm running with it. Next move.

Prince blew that song that was very appropriate for the evening, you know the one "If Eye Was the Man in Ur Life." No, I ain't no punk, but I do know how to treat a woman. I'm not down with giving every woman I court my precious jewels. I just have this feeling that she would be well worth my jewels.

When Prince was blowing that song, I wrapped my arms around her like she was already mine. She felt so good in my arms. We partied until what seemed like the break of dawn.

The concert was over at 11 p.m. The garden was packed, but we managed to stay in our spot without being pushed back. Okay, I didn't tell her that I had connections. We were able to talk to the Purple Badness himself for at least 30 minutes and he invited us up to his crib the next time that I was in town. He actually thought me and Femme were a couple. Not yet, but I was working on that.

I didn't want her to think that I was a crazy and deranged dude that just come up off the street trying to pick her up and things. I'm not the flowers and candy type dude. I like to smile and if I can give you a smile and you smile back, I've done my job. Little by little, day by day, Femme forgot about Mo. She even stopped accepting his calls. If what she was trying to do was get him to call more often, it worked, but by then her eyes were looking in another direction. I thought it was going to take forever for her to get over Mo. Every once in a while, she would bring it up and like a dutiful guy, I sat there and listened to her heart in pain. I tried everything whenever she got to that point to keep her mind off Mo.

Whenever there was a concert in town, we were there. I just made sure that Mo was in the back of her mind and that he stayed there.

One night, we were at this joint with good food. As we were getting ready to sit down, Femme spotted Mo across the way with this other chick. Believe this or not, he excused himself and headed toward the back. Femme's cell phone rang--it was Mo. She didn't answer, she chose to listen to his message and after she listened to the message, she actually let me hear it.

"This is Mo. I've been trying to call you for the longest time. I want to get together with you tonight so that we can talk. I'm ready to talk. I'm at work right now but I will call you back in an hour."

We laughed at the message and she deleted the message. We knew that it would be rude to do it, but we wanted to show him that he had been busted and now I, Cornelius, had all her time.

We walked casually over to Mo's table, and he looked as if

he had seen a ghost and he then dropped his head. We greeted the both of them and he managed to get a "hello" out of his mouth. Femme spoke politely and said her goodbyes; I laughed at the brother because he couldn't say that she was cheating because he was the one who stopped answering her calls. Now she knows the truth, she could move on, and move on with me she did.

The love was unbelievable. I see why Mo was probably so scared to commit. Femme put it down like there was no problem. She put something on me that I can't even explain. I'm not calling it a 'Love Jones' or nothing. She had me calling out to the high Heavens to have mercy on me and my heart. A brother now knows why Mo wasn't doing what he was supposed to do. He wasn't sure that he could give back the love that Femme gave out. Man, the lady was hardcore with her love. Get your mind out of the gutter. I'm not talking about that kind of hardcore loving. I'm talking about that kind of love that is given to a man to make that man say, "Uh huh, this is the sweet kind of love that I can't let go of." This was the kind of love that outside of the bedroom, she did things for you that was supposed to be done by the guy. She was definitely a keeper.

Mo wasn't for her. Why couldn't he see that? I'm not just talking about the lovemaking. I'm talking about the love she can give. When she loves, she loves damn hard. So, hard that a man like me can't catch his breath. I mean, I've had to pinch myself because she is so unreal, and I have her. She is amazing! You know a brother can screw up a wet dream and this sister would be right there to clean it up. She is Heaven sent, and I thought I would never find anybody like her. I thought I wasn't worthy of that kind of love. And I gave it back to her right. I came correct with mine. Whatever baby girl wanted, she got. Mo's loss and my gain.

I have uncovered a diamond.

CHAPTER 7

Ayanna

I was all about MA'AT and JAH and didn't give anyone a chance to really get to know me. I had my secrets that I didn't want to open myself to the ones even in my group. They didn't need to know what I do daily. I thought I was happy with my inner being but, there is always someone who wants to disrupt that inner peace. I light my incense, lay out my beads and cowl. One, I kneel to meditate, close my eyes and go inside myself, I felt MA'AT all over me, speaking to me, telling me I was the best, and the daughter of culture. Use this knowledge to control your destiny. I take time out each day when my soul has been disturbed. If it has been disturbed all day, then I spend all day until my spirit is calm enough to the point my spirit doesn't feel anything. Not even pain. JAH steps in and gives me extra peace, and protects me from dangers on the outside. Praise be MA'AT and JAH for life, those who don't know any better because if it weren't for them, I wouldn't know you. You would think headmasters know better and me to know the difference. He said it was in the powers that be MA'AT's way.

Being the new face in town, I thought I would never find a

place that shared the same views as me, but I did. Even now, I still take my time to meditate by myself because when others are involved, it throws off the alignment of the universe that you are trying to create so, I chose to meditate by myself.

I followed my father into the belief of MA'AT. I chose to stay with it after he went to prison to remain strong for him. Pops had the audacity to say that MA'AT let him down, but I believe he let MA'AT down. What he went to jail for is not to be discussed, but I will tell you this, he had no business doing what he did; he should look at it as being that he let MA'AT down. JAH, on the other hand, punished him, and he just couldn't see it. Daily I spent with MA'AT so that my universe around me could be in line and stay that way. There would always be something or someone to come in and make things different for that universe. I made the mistake of letting the headmaster in figuratively speaking. I let him come into me. I believed him. He told me what he was told. He was headmaster. I don't care if you are a grown woman or man when it's not consensual, it's not of MA'AT.

When I came to my senses, I prayed against the headmaster. It was my fault for letting him in. It was as if I was brainwashed. Other people would say that it was a cult, but I don't believe it was if I'm not worshipping with anybody else, but myself, right? The headmaster would stop by on occasion to make sure that I was doing what I was supposed to be doing. I thought it was very kind of him to come by and check on me seeing that I really didn't know much about my new surroundings. No one told me about the headmaster, and how he was.

He uses whatever spirituality that a person is into at the time just to get his fill. So, was he truly a headmaster? He went as far as starting his own MA'AT temple just to get me there and getting other people to join as well. He had some type of influence because when I decided to join, there were at least 50 people in the temple. I know that a person has to have a license, and other things to operate a temple, church, synagogue, or whatever you want to call where you worship. How the headmaster got all that up so quickly blows me away. The saddest part about all of it was that I had no one to tell. We walk around like we can do everything that the worldly people do, but I was scared to death of the headmaster because he threatened to hurt me even worse if I told. Did he get his in the end? Never mind that, this is about me, my sanity and my universe. So, I took what I learned and didn't return to what I used to call home. I couldn't go back there knowing what I knew about the headmaster, and wondering how many others has he done this to? MA'AT spoke to me and proclaimed that I didn't need to worry about him, that I would be well taken care of, he would get his, and JAH would make me stronger in the days to come.

With that power invested in me, that was given, I rented my clothes, purchased new ones, closed out everyone on the outside world, didn't eat for days, meditated to the Most High, gave all that I could to be me again, and now I'm whole.

I only give away the Precious Jewels to my mind to MA'AT and JAH.

CHAPTER 8

Jenny

Quo was my sidekick and Lynnette was my backbone. I, to them, was their road dog. I'd always go pick Quo up first so that I could give Lynnette time to get her bearings together. So what if I came from a well to do family. Those two were the only ones who didn't mind me rolling like I rolled when I wanted to. Even when it was late at night, when I needed to bounce, I bounced. I made sure that I had my stash with me so, we could coast on 9th Street for the rest of the evening. I didn't want to get into any trouble, and I wasn't about to go and get my dogs in trouble neither.

I think Quo has a thing for me. He's always making those puppy dog eyes at me. Lynnette would always tell me that he did have a thing for me just because I had something that no other female had. What it was? I don't know. I mean, I'm just an average chick from around the way, right? Quo was my boy though. He was a straight fool when it came to cursing people out when they stepped to me or Lynnette wrong. He was just that kind of protective. I had some cash flow on me so, I decided we'd all make a night of it away from home. We strolled to the other side of town after picking up Lynnette.

I told the both of them, "Look, I got me some cash flow and we can go to the Marriott on Memorial Drive. I don't want to go back home tonight. Do y'all have any plans for tomorrow?"

They both shook their heads no, and we kept rolling. Made a stop off at Dominoes, KFC, and Lucky 7. We had the works Pizza, chicken, and fish with dessert, of course, and a two-liter soda.

We checked in, took a deep breath, and started in on our food. Quo pulled from his coat pocket the stash that we had from last week, lit an incense, lit up the stash and passed it around as we ate the pizza, the chicken, and the fish. We knew by the end of the night, we would have to go back out and get something else to grub on. Was it fair for us to ruin our bodies the way we did? It's not like we did it every day. It was only when we felt like doing it.

Upon meeting Lynnette, I thought she was stuck up, but come to find out, she was very down to earth. I met Lynnette at some kind of meet up gig in town one evening 7 years ago, and as she puts it, "I like what I see." We've been hanging together since. I trusted her with everything that I had. I even let her drive my car. As I stated, I knew we were going to have the munchies afterwards so, I let Lynnette borrow the car to go get us something more to eat on. This time, she chose the place. Quo and I stayed in the room because he said that he had something to talk to me about. Lynnette looked at me with those eyes, turned and walked out the door. As I got comfortable in the reclining chair the hotel had in the room, I propped my legs open like I was a boy, and one of Quo's boys. He really didn't appreciate the fact that I did that around him and he so desperately wanted me to change the way I carried myself when I was around him. *"Say what!"* Brother has me twisted if he thinks I'm going to change for him, or anybody else for that matter.

Right then and there he stood up, grabbed me by the hand, and pulled me up to him. Next thing I know Quo and I are locking lips like it was natural for us to be doing that, and like we've been doing that all along. Naw, this can't be happening. But it was, and I had to come to grips with the fact that Lynnette wasn't lying. I never realized how I long for a man to embrace me. My father never hugged me so, I didn't know what it meant to be held. So, I just let the stuff happen like it was supposed to happen. I kissed back thinking that Quo really wouldn't have responded, but he did. He held me tighter. It's amazing how a person's body and even the lips can match. Quo eased me onto the bed where he proceeded to take my clothes off, as I did to him.

Things started to get heated when Lynnette came back in, but for some reason, we didn't stop. Lynnette casually closed the door, put the food down, and watched the both of us while we groped each other. Lynnette stood up and began to take off her clothes. We stopped kissing to wait on her to join us.

Lynnette knew all along that Quo wanted me and I didn't want to believe her, but she too wanted me. Now that, I did not know. Quo laid on his back as I sat on him in the cowgirl position. Lynnette came up behind me and started stroking me. What a unique feeling this was because two people wanted me. It scared me at first, but they both assured me that everything was going to be all right. What shocked me was the fact that both Quo and Lynnette felt good to me, and I began to get real comfortable with what was going on. Quo never touched Lynnette and Lynnette never touched Quo, and I wondered why.

They both had their reason for not touching each other and both of their reasons was the same. They each wanted to please me. Quo watched as Lynnette pleasured me and Lynnette watched as Quo pleased me. It seemed to last for hours, but we weren't going anywhere until the morning. Lynnette laid on the bottom, I was in the middle and Quo was on top this time. I felt him go deep inside me and the sound that I made turned Lynnette on and she wanted in on the action. She turned over underneath me to face me and begin to play with me. This feeling of ecstasy took me to a level that I had never experienced before. It was like a Samantha type thing that I couldn't get rid of. I blamed it on being high, and that had nothing to do with it. I loved the both of them and wanted them equally, and all to myself.

I know what you're thinking, "She's bisexual."

At that particular time, I wouldn't say that I was, but after that night, I had to make a decision. I would either choose Quo and have a boyfriend, or choose Lynnette and have a girlfriend, either one I choose and lose both, but I couldn't have both. Or could I? Now I'm walking on dangerous territory. I do believe that Quo thought Lynnette would stay out a little longer. It could have been planned that way. If Quo had gone and got the food, Lynnette and I probably would have been doing that too.

It was me and my dogs. People wondered why they never saw us with anybody else. It was just me, Quo and Lynnette all. . .the. . .time. I knew Quo loved me and I knew Lynnette loved me. Would there be a fight if I chose just one? Did they really not like each other? It was time to find out the truth. I switched positions so that Lynnette and Quo would be facing each other. Lynnette felt his manhood, but it didn't feel right to her. She likes the fact that he was cute and all, but she didn't want him. She wanted Quo to want me and Quo did. Quo wanted Lynnette to want me. They hugged, and both raised up to look at me.

They were thinking the same thing. Things don't have to change, it will just be our little secret. I slept in between them.

CHAPTER 9

Tina

I woke up looking at a bright light and this funny stench entered my nose. Trying to gather my bearings to remember what happened, I coughed, but couldn't move my hands *BECAUSE* I was strapped to a flatbed. The doctor came in saying that the team has pumped my stomach because I had digested three bottles of Cyclobenzaprine when all I was trying to do was get rid of the pain and go to sleep. I wasn't supposed to live and whoever found me is going to get a good butt kicking when I see them. My neighbors don't have no business popping up on my doorstep wanting anything from me. . .especially calling themselves saving my life. Did it ever occur to them that I wanted to die?

I don't have anything to my name. Everyone around me has *something*. I'm not saying that I didn't work hard to get where I am. I suppose in my quest for greatness, I wanted a lot more than what I had. Doesn't everybody want more? I mean, sure, yeah, I had a decent job that I was happy with or it made me happy, a roof over my head, and a dog to keep me company. I really don't like to answer to anybody. That's why I remained single. Who in the world is going to want my old behind? I can

The Precious Jewels Monologue

sniff out a dude a mile away who's just wanting a roll in the sack. I am nobody's cow. My little theory is that when a man wants you, he's going to do everything in his power to get to where you are at all times, and if the guy is not a stalker or you can tolerate him then hey! Go for what you know. But I am sick and tired of being somebody's car wheel.

Okay, let me explain this car wheel theory to you for those of you who fix flats. When you're on a flat, you either purchase a new tire or try to fix the one you already have. You pay special attention to what happened to that tire if you're willing to keep it and make it look brand new. So, you take this tire, right? And you look at the damage it may have caused by taking it out a lot or not checking on it from time to time. You go and you put some type of calking on the tire to cover the damaged area. But then once that's done, you continue to treat that tire as you did earlier on, right? Then you end up having to purchase new tires anyway. Now, see I've just compared a relationship to tires. How long do tires last? That's how long a relationship lasts for me. . .maybe even not that long. I've gotten to the point in my life where I'm saying, "Screw all those who didn't screw with me." I was the best thing that could ever happen to Cecil, Dexter, Marvin, Jericho, Oscar,

Wayne, and Steven. I was tired of being treated like one of the boys. I AM A WOMAN!

I had more shoes in my closet than money in my bank account, but I made mine. I wasn't really living paycheck to paycheck so, how did I end up here in this hospital room, lying on a hospital bed? I didn't go out to a club and meet nobody, nor did I have company over. The doctor said that I digested some pills. I don't believe that I could do such a thing, but knowing me, yes, I probably did. Hospital bed or no hospital bed, I wanted out. I wanted out of the hospital, out of myself and out of this place. The place where I live inside my head. Some days it would be too full and the other days, it would feel too empty.

A year ago, I decided to close myself off to the world because I felt that I didn't owe the world anything and just for that, the world took my mind. No, not like an alien abduction. I was crying and screaming too much. I often wondered why my family never came to visit me. I suppose that was a good thing that they didn't.

I lived a normal life as far as keeping my house clean, and people who came to visit when I did have visitors, talked about me behind my back saying that I was anal. . .Anal? Just because

I like to keep my house clean, I'm anal? Man! People have life all screwed up and they want to call me crazy. Oh yeah, crazy. . .I have the papers to prove it. They put me through a series of tests, and those psychiatrists just couldn't see what I was seeing so they stamped an insane on my wrist and threw me in solitaire. For days, I didn't eat because I was trying to prove a point, and they still didn't listen. Being in that place alone is enough to drive a person mad. You become set apart from the world and then you're on your own in trying to figure out what's real and what's not. So, I remain in my own little world because, in my little world, I survived whatever those doctors put on me.

They said that I had a relapse. Which I know that is a lie because I was just in pain. Nothing was whispering in my ear telling me to take all the pills. I just felt that people would be better off without me here. . .I'd be better off if I could just get some sleep. Was there anything in my childhood to make me be this way? Not that I can recall. My mother was never beaten by my father, my father always came home for dinner and never went back out; and he actually gave mother his paycheck and kept $100--imagine that. So, what happened to me? Life. It threw me a biscuit and I wanted caviar. And I can't stand the smell of it. I know what you're thinking, you're thinking, well, how are you now? I get tested every six months to see how well my progression is as far as living.

I still don't want anyone approaching me. Then I remembered as a little girl this huge Bible on my auntie's mantle. All she would say to me is "Child read." Then it occurred to me that she had gone through the same thing I did, but no one told me. She passed away 10 years ago.

I found my Bible and turned to Mark 5:9-15. This is the story of Legion. Not DaNisha's Legion, I don't know why anyone would name their child that. But he seemed like his story was the same as the one in the Bible. He was that man who was cutting himself but recognized Jesus as being the Son of the Most High God. It's amazing that even demons know who Jesus is. This thing that had a hold on me was an unclean spirit and I had to realize that. That's why my auntie always told me to read. My mind is straight because Jesus had compassion on me.

CHAPTER 10

Sasha

All I wanted was a husband. A man that was going to love me just as much as I loved him. I got sick and tired of dealing with these online dating sites that didn't even give me good results. I changed up my profile many times just to receive a positive companion. I didn't lie about myself; I had no reason to. I am a successful businesswoman with much to hold down. I just wanted someone I can share my success with. Is that too much to ask for? I'm not going to give you the sob story of how I grew up, what I wanted out of life, how I was going to raise my children if I ever had any because that would take up too much time and I'm sure you are not here to listen to me rant and rave about what had gone on in my past.

I've worked hard to get to where I am today, and I didn't have to step on anybody's toes to get there. My friend Josh of many years helped me through a difficult situation, so why wasn't I with him? He didn't like me that way, or so I thought. You would think that he would have told me something earlier on, right? I'm near 50 with one foot in the grave. No man wants a woman my age. They tend to look at younger women with a fresher look. So, I went out and started doing things for myself.

Not that I was helpless. My mother always told me that I shouldn't depend on a man doing things for me. Was she right? Now you and I both know that there are things we cannot do as women since we are supposed to be the weaker vessels.

It has been at least five years since Josh and I lost contact with each other. This man was the epitome of the man that I fixed up in my dreams, but I just never knew what it was about me that didn't cause him to step up like I wanted him to. I checked myself once over to see if I had everything in tow. I didn't look half bad, had a good education, a home, a business, and no children. Did I intimidate him? If I did, he never told me. I kept myself looking decent whenever I went out. We shared things. This man was and still is my best friend. I could tell him everything. And dealing with other men if he was bothered by it, he sure didn't let on that it bothered him. The best types of relationships come from being the best of friends. Wasted time was all that was. And at that time, Josh was going through his own issues. You know men always want to fix things and don't ever think a woman won't ever be there for them to cry on their shoulders. If more men would say how they hurt, we both would get along so much better. That's just my opinion.

The Precious Jewels Monologue

With that, the men wouldn't want to seem like wimps around women. I would love it if a man would cry in front of me. That only shows me that the man has a heart. But please don't take it to the extent of turning it into a pity party PLEASE! It took me forever to leave my pity party, get up on my feet and start brand new. When I found myself, started loving myself, I was able to allow love to come in and sup with me, and me with love. The day I saw Josh cry was the day my whole world changed. He came to me with a situation, and I politely listened. What was I to say to this beautiful man? Every woman was after this guy, but yet, he chose to spend his undying hours with me. His situation wasn't a job or his education. His situation was another woman. I knew about her and she knew we were friends.

He spent money like water running on this woman. Granted, she was beautiful, but even the most beautiful person can be ugly on the inside. We spent hours in conversation and an hour in sheer silence because I couldn't find the words to console him. There are times when words are not meant to be said; a person just needs to be listened to. When he took his last breath to exhale, the tears began to flow and all I could do was hold him. He seemed to cry for more hours into the night. It was a good thing that I didn't have to open up the next morning. I planned a get-a-way just the two of us and had my assistant, Stacie take over for the next few days. She is a good worker and she deserves a raise for all the things she has pulled me out of.

I booked a trip to Hawaii for myself and Josh and made sure he had some time he could use to take off. We spent a week in Hawaii. I'm glad I booked that trip because we both needed it. I closed out all my dating web accounts, packed a bag and jetted to Hawaii for some sun and relaxation. Josh and I had adjoining rooms so that if he ever couldn't sleep, he could always wake me up. It seemed that he spent more time in my suite more than he did his. I've always enjoyed spending time with Josh, but I never thought I would take it as far as to get him away from everything. I did it without thinking because I considered him to be my best friend.

When we returned from Hawaii, he had a new outlook on life, and he kept saying, *"All because of you Boo, all because of you."* I thought nothing of it. He asked me out to dinner one night but, the catch was--he cooked. I'm thinking that it was just a friendly dinner to thank me for all that I had done for him but, he had done just as much for me. It was a good thing that I came dressed to the nines. You know, with an evening dinner, it's usually a black dress and that's what I wore. He was dressed in his best attire and there was really no dress code.

Well, on into dinner, he stopped to look at me, and I wondered why he was looking at me so hard. He had my favorite: smothered pork chops, stewed vegetables, grilled mushrooms, and a salad with vinaigrette dressing. I told him that dinner was excellent and that I didn't know that he could throw down the way he did. And when Josh smiles that king smile, it always made me melt and my toes curl. He didn't seem nervous at all as he cleared his throat and chewed the last piece of chop on his plate.

"Sasha, you've been there for a brother since the beginning and in turn, I did my best to be there for you. With all the women in the world that I have dealt with, you are the one who stood back to let me make my mistakes and didn't dog me out about it but comforted me when my heart was breaking. You didn't know as well as I didn't know. Sasha, the love of my life, would you do me the honor of being my wife?"

"Yes."

CHAPTER 11

Jasmine

I spent my days sitting in class wondering if this man was ever going to give up the other life that he claimed that he told me he was going to give up. At some point in my life, I don't know what he saw in me, but whatever it was, it must have been good because anything that I needed, he was there to supply it. It wasn't as if I needed anything because with schooling came having a job, and a good one at that. I thought so anyway because I was doing what my heart wanted to do plus with the help of God. Okay, sure, I'm putting God in my life because I've been in some horrible situations and I knew I had to get out of that situation. I didn't want to live like that for the rest of my natural life, but what I'm doing is really no better than what I'm doing now.

So, sitting in class learning the trade of becoming a nail technician. . .call me ghetto if you want, but that's what I want to do, I get paid nicely, my clientele is on the top list, and where I work, they want me to come in because I bring in the customers. So, you may ask what is it that I do that is so wrong? The man I'm with is married. My daddy taught me better than that, but goodness, he was a bad example, bringing in women out on the street that he claimed he was helping. With what? Okay, so daddy wasn't married, but he dealt with married women. Maybe he thought that because they were married, he wouldn't have to bother with them staying. These women would have a place to go home to, even though their husbands weren't getting the job done, so they picked on my dad for convenience.

I'm a little rough around the edges. . .ghetto fabulous, if you will. The thing that I don't do is walk around acting like I'm all that and a bag of chips. It took me forever or what seemed like forever to get to where I am, and I didn't need to step on anybody's toes to get there. But this married man! Oooooooweee! He just makes my toes curl. I know it's wrong, but like daddy, I don't have to deal with him on a regular basis. My thought is though, *"why did he choose me to fool around with?"* I wasn't even in the market to look for someone. I said to myself that my heart was fixed, and my mind is made up so, what am I missing? My own man. I don't want to live like my daddy did and have someone else's something. That's just nasty, but I'm doing it anyway. I want my own, but I realize that even before me there was someone else, and praying that I don't pay for the sins of the other which often times men make

The Precious Jewels Monologue

us do.

Not to say that women make men pay for the other's mistakes, but that's life, and we will never understand each other. The last man I was with belong to me, but I just wasn't enough for him. Each time I told him that I loved him, his response to me would be "ditto." At first, I thought it was cute, but then I realized that he was saving the "I love's you" for someone else. It took me all of six months to realize that the relationship that I dreamed of was going nowhere so, I decided not to ever deal with another heartbreak again and only deal with married men. As I've stated, they. . .go. . .home. I don't care about their jobs nor do I accept gifts from them. There are seven days in a week, 12 hours in a day, the sun goes down at 5:34 p.m. and rise at 7:04 a.m. I get my rest, enjoy my days, work at noon and cry at night. I have a full plate. Yeah, yeah, you've heard that when people say they don't have time to date, what they are actually saying is that there is no one of their calibers to date them. You have all the time in the world to date if you want to, you just don't. I'll make time. I'll just have to change the rules of the game. It's my play and I'm the one who is supposed to be in control, right? I attract these married men like bees to honey.

All I do is smile to let people know that I notice them. It seems like not a day goes by that I'm not smiling. I have to smile to hide the pain. The pain of not wanting to deal with another married man for as long as I live. What's keeping me from saying "NO?" My mind. I guess it all boils down to the fact that I don't want to feel lonely. I just don't like that feeling. So, going out, I found it to be easy. Sitting at the bar, I noticed that when a man comes up, I check out the ring finger. I've become adamant about men without the print of the ring on his finger. Those that aren't married will not tell you that they have a significant other waiting at home for them. I would give just about anything to have that special someone in my life that I can wait at home for. And for him to open the door to our place and say, "Honey, I'm hoooome." Those are the magical words a man could utter coming out of his mouth, and then to plant a sweet tender kiss on those subtle lips! Lord, help my time, but my time is not His time you see. So, at this point in my life, I'm in my season. Where that season leads me, I don't know so, I'll wait and pray and wait some more. Will I ever get tired of waiting? Maybe. My mind can't take too much more waiting on someone who may or may be worth my time.

I opened the door to my place, "Aaaaahhhh, solace."

CHAPTER 12

Stacie

It has been 19 years, and I can still hear Michael whispering to me as he put his stubby hands on my breasts.

"You know you want me inside of you."

He proceeded to move his hands in different directions, and then to the inside of my pants. I screamed, telling him to stop, but he wouldn't listen. The kitchen sink was cold to the front of my body as he continued to force himself inside of me. I pleaded with him to stop. He still wouldn't. He became a monster, someone I didn't know anymore.

His hands reached around my neck, and he said in a deep raspy voice, "Continue to scream. No one is going to hear you, and if you tell, no one will believe you. I'll say I was with my boys. Especially if you tell, I will come back and finish the job. You scream one more time, I'm going to break your neck."

Ten minutes later, he backed away breathless, laughed and told me, "You know you wanted this big piece of meat." His face, vulgar. His demeanor, proud. His eyes light brown and shark-like with a nasty superior grin. This man of African-American Caucasian descent stood 5'7" with a Michelin-man

The Precious Jewels Monologue

body behind me with no remorse.

On a warm Tuesday afternoon April 21, 1992, my life and soul became lost. After he left, I slowly walked to the bathroom, sore, confused and frightened. I was bleeding. I became distant and quiet. I pretended it never happened. Even though I had a boyfriend, this other man violated me. I blocked that day out of my mind. I didn't tell my boyfriend because I didn't know what he would think of me.

My boyfriend had accused me of sleeping with another man, and I hadn't. Michael was an old friend that I came to trust again. The day "it" happened, he said that he couldn't stay away. What led him to do what he did? I have no answer to that question. I told my former boyfriend a year later. My boyfriend told me that if in fact, it happened, it was something that I had to deal with on my own, and he would do what he could to make me feel better. I told two of my family member months after the incident. All they could do was apologize. The trauma ate me up inside for many years, and I didn't know what to do. I couldn't bring myself to go to a counselor because I felt ashamed. And I didn't want to tell my mother what happened because she liked Michael.

Rape for me was a frightening experience. My life was

threatened because of not only his words but also, his actions. I received some information from my friend on rape when I went to visit her. She was the backbone of the support I needed. Every once in a while, the nightmare comes back to haunt me which makes me have to start all over again to have a peace of mind.

It took many years for me to break the silence, and come to terms with the rape. Through prayer and meditation, I've learned to breathe again.

CANVAS

On

PRECIOUS JEWELS

CANVAS

The light bulb went out in the darkroom

So that's why you had to be moved

To

A secluded place

I love the way you flatter me in the moonlight

Yet the essence of your colors

Look like the sun on fire surrounded by

Stars with icicles

Image that...

I breathe in your oils that are mixed

With Jojoba and Chamomile

The aroma made my body float

As I stood

Back and let the colors

Fly

And I remained

Still...

The beauty enlightened my mind

As the paint seems to

Travel making its own

Pattern

Enlarging an area that took

Days to create

I

Succumbed to the inside

Of you

As I closed my eyes

I was no more...

CHAPTER 13

Peter

I make my own self-sick sometimes the way I treat women, but they make it so easy. I have a way of breaking down women if they are already not broken down. I scope out those I can really intimidate, charm, get them to tell me all their secrets and then BOOM! I hit them with *"Is it all right if we just have sex"* line? Usually by then, they would have fallen for me deep enough that they are not able to pull away. I consider myself to be a fairly handsome guy. Okay, I want to blame that on my mother, but I won't. She always told me I was her prince and women would fall at my feet if I treated them right. I know I'm not Jesus, but she never taught me **how** to treat a woman. I'm the biggest whore around you ever want to meet. No, it's not funny, but I had to laugh at that comment. It's not like I planned on being that way. I just love. . .sex. And sex loves me. You would think that all the sex I've had, I would have caught something by now, right? WRONG! I made sure that once I got to know these women, we both go get tested. See, I wanted them to trust me enough so that I could get at them. You know, make it look like I really cared about their well-being. Melissa was fine as chocolate ice

The Precious Jewels Monologue

cream on a summer day. I hit that twice a week. Japhari was literally my African queen, but all she wanted to do was get high and drink, so I knew I was in. Dahlia was too quiet for words which made me feel like I wasn't hitting it right, but I made sure she was satisfied outside of the bedroom. Olivia was my sweet pea. We both had that insatiable appetite, and she knew I was dealing with other women. She didn't seem to mind. Diamond always wanted to prove a point which ended up in physical fights. I didn't realize until later that fighting with her was a huge turn on for her that led to sex. It became addictive. Selah frightened me just because of her name. Yes, I know my Bible just like I know my God, but even the devil was God's right-hand morning star. So. . .what?! I fell from grace. Everybody falls short. I'm trying to get back to being in His good graces. Selah made it so hard for me to do that. My mind was constantly on getting to **know** her. And I did. She wasn't the perfect little angel everyone thought she was. I had her climbing that walls. She was the main one stroking my. . .ego making me feel like the man I desired to be. She called me "her Spiderman." Okay, so my last name is Parker and I got teased a lot in school about it. My mom and dad were huge fans of Spiderman back in the day. They met at a Spiderman convention. Nicholas Hammond, the actor who played Spiderman, was a big part of their lives. I grew to love Spiderman. Once married, they said they would name their son Peter. I know, that's so bland, but the story excites me every time I hear it. I know Selah can't save me from myself. She can't be my superhero. I have to want it for myself. If there was ever a chance to get with her, make her mine and only mine, I would. . .if she'd have me.

And then there's Damika. She was just a gorgeous BBW. I went out of my way to impress the living daylights out of her. Was she impressed? I had this woman paying my rent for God's sake! Not that I couldn't pay my own rent, she wanted to. I'm real estate. Nice home, cool ride, money to spend ridiculously if I wanted to, but I don't. I have money in the bank and offshore accounts. It wasn't easy though. I worked my way to the top. Damika was another kind-hearted female who bent over backward just to please me. She cleaned my house. What man wouldn't want that? She was doing wifely duties knowing full well I was never going to wife her. I broke down and had to tell her that "I just don't see us walking down the aisle in holy matrimony. I don't hear wedding bells." Yeah, I'm sure that hurt her, but she needed to know. It seemed to make her work harder at pleasing me. Then, I got a wakeup call. She came in with a few of her male friends one night and took out everything she had purchased for me. I stood there looking bewildered, wondering why she was doing all of that. And she reminded me.

And last, but not least, Antoinette. Sounds sexy doesn't she? As fine as the day the doctor slapped her on her behind sexy. There are no words to describe how this woman made *me* climb the walls. She had me going crazy because I only got the chance to see her once a week. That shouldn't have bothered me because I had my other honeys to keep me satisfied, or so I thought. Antoinette was poison. Unlike like the others who were toxic to me, this woman had me searching in the dark for a flashlight. You just had to be there to know how bad ass she was. Instead of me charming her, she charmed the pants right off of me. No, I'm not saying that she took me for all I'm worth, I'm saying that she had me so wrapped up in her that I didn't want to deal with the others. Had I, Peter Parker, fallen for the real okie doke? Was she evil? Was she a witch that cast a spell on me, or was it simply that I had fallen in love?

You may be wondering how I divided my time up with all of them. There really was no dividing them up. A few would come

The Precious Jewels Monologue

on the same nights. I would just pretend that I had no company, and do the same thing all over again with each woman every week. Then there would be times when I would see them one night a week. I found it easy to break up my time. Of course, as I stated, they all knew about each other. Antoinette could have gotten anything out of me if she wanted to.

I guess I'll never know even though I bit, she bit back. Seven months in and I had all the women surrounding me at once. They all knew of one another because I made it a point not to hide anything from them. They seemed cordial to one another. The one face I was grateful to see was Selah. I needed her at that moment. To each woman, I told how I felt, and what each one meant to me. I honestly thought I was doing right by them, by bringing them together. I have no idea what they will do after they leave. They gathered around me, showered me with kisses and hugs and with tears in their eyes said, "I love you." Selah suggested praying. What a relief to hear her say that. They joined hands in prayer, and as Selah prayed for deliverance, I closed my eyes hoping that I was back in God's good grace.

I am Peter "Spiderman" Parker.

CHAPTER 14

Mecca

My Godmother gave me that name thinking that I would be a blessing to the world. Boy was she wrong! To some, I was an angel, but I was only hiding behind something that I couldn't fight. Maybe I didn't want to fight. My bestie used to say, "Something is seriously wrong with you." all because I cracked jokes that no one has ever heard of or talk like it ain't nobody's business but my own. I just wanted to see people smile and laugh. And when I see that, then I know I've done a good thing. And I don't have to be high to do it either. But I love getting high. Not on the hard stuff. I just don't see how the people who do the hard stuff, can handle that. I hate to sneeze. That literally hurts.

My life wasn't hard so to speak. I just made it that way. I ran away from home a lot. My mom was on that stuff and my dad was in prison for selling. I love my weed. It calms me when I don't want to deal with the world or my mother. Get this: I even hold down a job. This guy by the name of Bryce Stillmore just out of the blue offered me a job working at his computer software company on the west side. He was saying that he was thinking about expanding his brand and taking it global all

The Precious Jewels Monologue

because he saw me work a Sudoku puzzle. I was like "Hell man! Anybody can work a Sudoku puzzle." He clapped back saying that he couldn't. He figured that I was good at math just because of that.

This man went out of his way to take me shopping for some new digs just, so I could look professional coming into work. He was already impressed by the puzzle so, I was a shoe-in for the job. Learning the technical stuff should be a breeze. Anything to get away from my mother. All I could do was pray for her. The funds would give me the chance to move into my own place. Having my own place was already taken care of. Bryce. . .Mr. Stillmore had that already set up and a company car. Wow! God had blessed me so much to get out from under my mother, and try to help her get better that I didn't stop to thank Him. Even though I held onto my weed, I continued to thank Him for everything. Mr. Stillmore knew about my smoking, and he hired me anyway.

He said, "As long as it doesn't affect your ability to concentrate on the task at hand."

HA! Does he not know about Mary Jane? Okay, so I don't smoke 24/7. I smoke to ease pain and forget about things when I feel like the world is on my shoulders. Why is it that now

The Precious Jewels Monologue

whenever I smoke, I read my Bible? That is so ironic. What's even more ironic is I know that when you read, God is speaking to you.

I never fought God's love. The fact is you would think I would be angry with Him for putting me with parents who had no business having me in the first place. My Godmother once told me that I was put here for a reason. I'm still trying to figure out that reason. Mr. Stillmore wanted me now to keep an eye on his wife. What does it look like me keeping an eye on his wife? He must think she's cheating or something. But she was working at his company as well. Each day she left, I had to pretend as though I was going to run an errand, I would follow her and report back to Mr. Stillmore. Nothing to be wetting his lips over. She wasn't seen with another man, or looking suspicious coming out of the bank. This one particular day, I seen her with this young man; he was mad gorgeous. Surely, she wasn't stepping out on him. I proceeded to take pictures and report back to Mr. Stillmore.

A weeks worth of keeping an eye on Mrs. Stillmore, things didn't change. The meeting with this young man continued and the lunch always ended with a hug and kiss on the cheek. Mr. Stillmore was paranoid, so I went to his office, pulled out my

The Precious Jewels Monologue

trusted friend, and told him to relax. Wrong move. . .not that I lost my job, it just made him more paranoid. So, thinking innocently, I invited him over to the home he paid for, so he could just chill. He told Samantha that he was having to go over the account books for the six month period, so that I could be caught up with the company since I just started.

With account books in hand, Mr. Stillmore shows up at my front door ready to get to work. We spent four hours trying to get the books straight. He explained to me the variations of computer software, and how the accounts are tied into the business without it looking like a scam.

He wanted to know how Sudoku works, so I explained that to him. "Its a logic-based combinatorial number-placement puzzle. The objective is to fill a 9x9 grid with digits, so that each column, each row, and each of the 3x3 sub-grids that compose the grid contains all digits from 1 to 9. The puzzle setter provides a partial completed grid, which for a well-posed puzzle has a single solution."

You should have seen the look on his face when I finished explaining it to him. I ended up showing him how it's done.

Then he said, "Maybe I need to smoke one just to see if it would help me finish."

I was hesitant at first. It was the boss!

He said, "Come on, what could it hurt? I already know you do it. It's not like I'm going to fire you."

Against my better judgment, I fired one up in hopes that it wouldn't make him paranoid like the first time. He worked a puzzle all by himself and to him, that was cause for a celebration. What did he have in mind? A Pacific Veggie pizza and a bottle of Rotari Raspbericello. It was good that it was like that because, after smoking, we both got the munchies. He looked at me and started talking about how he wanted to do away with the guy his wife was seeing. I explained to him that it was unethical. She was supposed to be the love of his life. Why go to certain lengths to get rid of someone he doesn't know? I suggested he show her the pictures and ask who he was to her. Mr. Stillmore was dead set on doing away with this man.

I insisted that he do it my way; and if he finds that she is cheating, get a divorce, and give her half. He told me that he doesn't believe in divorce, and stated how much he loves this woman. Eating all of the extra-large pizza, and drinking the bottle of wine, I told him that he should stay in the other room to sleep it off. I was brought up with some common sense to know that you never drink and drive. I helped him to the bedroom, laid him down, and told him to rest well. I'm glad he slept it off and remembered where he was in the process.

He gathered his thoughts and within the next couple of days, he called me into his office to thank me for talking some sense into him. It turns out that the young man Mrs. Stillmore was meeting was her half-brother to discuss their father's will. She didn't seem upset that Mr. Stillmore had her followed, but that he didn't trust her enough. It was as if he didn't know her at all because she never talked about her half-brother. Mr. Stillmore told me in the beginning that I would be well taken care of and he kept his promise.

Five years later, he appointed me vice president of Stillmore Software for saving a man's life.

CHAPTER 15

Cobra

I woke up, stretched, yawn and scratched my head getting ready for the day. I turned around and noticed myself lying there...still. ***Am I dead?***

I stood there pondering and figuring out what I had done last night. Last night was really a blur considering that I don't drink or smoke. I couldn't necessarily call anyone to find out what happened. I do know that I wasn't with anyone. I took a deep breath, closed my eyes, counted to 20, opened my eyes and looked on the bed again. The body was still there.

"Oh, I'm dreaming."

I eased towards the door, not knowing what would be on the other side. And to my surprise after opening the door, I stepped on the sidewalk heading down to Fordham in the Bronx. I have no idea how I got there, but I was.

Then I remembered the body back in the bed, *"This is not real."* I almost panicked.

"Damn! Did it again."

Went to sleep and astral projected myself. I might as well enjoy this while I'm here. It was crazy though because I couldn't find one nail shop that I wanted to go to. Every shop I went into was a dungeon.

I took a deep breath, closed my eyes, and repeated, *"This is not real."*

I opened my eyes and I was back in my room. I wanted to wake up, but I wanted to see where I would go next. Realizing that I can't stay away too long, I really wanted to go back to New York to find a friend. I counted down from 20 and closed my eyes. Gasping for air, I sat up in bed collecting my thoughts. I sat up and looked around the room. Nothing seemed out of place or anything, so I planted my feet firmly on the floor.

"Yup, I'm awake."

Turning the knob and opening the door, I walked into the nail salon of my dreams.

"Damn, still sleep. Might as well get my nails done while I'm here."

I sat in the chair getting comfortable waiting for my turn. The woman walked up and asked me what I wanted done today? I told her an overlay and just work her magic. I looked up and it looked like I was staring into a mirror. I blinked once, and then again to make sure my eyes weren't playing tricks on me.

"This isn't real."

The nail tech didn't speak to me the whole time I was sitting in the chair. She just smiled. The nail tech seemed happy with her position and continued to work quietly. She had done such a wonderful job on my nails, I gave her a tip.

Upon leaving, I turned to her and asked her, "Why is it that you look so much like me?"

She responded, "Because I am you and you belong here."

I looked at her bewildered, bid her good day, walked outside and noticed the sign. . .**COBRA NAILS.**

CHAPTER 16

Rowan

I gave her my all, but she insisted on seeing other men who didn't mean her any good. One man got married on her and the other just wanted sex and nothing more. We even went on a trip together to get away from everything. She didn't tell the other two. There really was no need. I wanted to make this trip special for her even though she suggested the trip. It was much needed for the both of us. All I wanted to do was be with her.

Jessica was the love of my life. Or she is the love of my life, but she fails to see it. I would love it if, in the back of her mind, she felt the same. I called myself attempting to talk to her about it, but I suppose I didn't try hard enough. Jessica and I have been friends for a very long time, and when you see us together, you would think we were married. Here's the situation: I had other lady friends at the time and she understood my relationships. When they fell apart, she'd be the one who I'd run to when my heart was hurting. Not many people grabbed the concept of our relationship.

Just as I sat there listening to her rant and rave about her issues with men, she did the same for me. Okay, I must admit,

The Precious Jewels Monologue

after awhile, we did become intimate, but that didn't change or mess up our friendship. It was one of those nights where we kept each other company after our five initial dates. We both wanted to get the feel of if in fact, we could be friends with all the common interests we have. Jessica and I meshed so well together. I could see in her eyes that she wanted more, but I didn't want to push.

We literally had to find time for each other. Jessica was in real estate and I had my own graphic design company. That's how we met. I was looking for property and she was recommended by a good friend of mine. I called the number and spoke directly to her. Her voice was Heaven. We met for drinks later that day in October. I told her of my plans to expand years after I get started if my business was a success. I could tell as I was telling her all these things, the wheels in her head were turning with a lot of ideas. She knew exactly the place that would be perfect for me in the long run without breaking the bank to get it. After drinks, she drove me to the spot to show me the building she had in mind. I looked around and told her I would think about it. I was always taught not to jump at the first opportunity and asked if there were any other properties that I could take a look at if she had any more.

I offered to discuss other options over dinner, and she accepted. That's how we met. It was a business venture at first, but over time, I started having feelings for her. These men in her life took a jewel for granted, and she is allowing it to happen. I stood by and watched it happen. How am I to tell this woman how much I love her? Every time that thought creeps up, I shut down. This could be my own insecurities of being rejected. I should have more confidence in myself enough to tell the woman of my dreams, that I love her. Maybe she is waiting for me to just blurt it out. Men and women waste precious time not telling others how they feel about them. I've gotten to know Jessica pretty well, so I see no need to not tell her how I feel.

The question is, *"will she feel the same?"*

It's now or never. Date night time! I called her up, told her that I wanted to take her out and be ready by 7:30. I dressed up in my finest clothes, washed my car and purchased a bouquet of flowers. I come correct with mine. I was as nervous as a school kid on his first date. I made it to her place on time. Rang the doorbell, and when she opened the door with a smile on her face, I knew things would be all right. We both complimented each other, I handed her the flowers, sat down as she put them in water. She positioned herself beside me and continued to smile. God, that smile!

We had reservations, so we made our way to the car. I opened the door for her and helped her inside. The ride was a bit quiet on the way there, but I finally broke the silence. It was time.

"I would like to tell you something."

CHAPTER 17

Chae Ann

I was sitting at the bar when I was approached by this dude. He continued to be a nuisance when I told him that I really didn't want to be bothered tonight. Why is it that men can't get the hint whenever they see a fine woman in their presence? Just by the looks alone, he couldn't tell that I wanted to be left alone. I had a bad day, and all I wanted was some time to myself. Maybe some parts of me wanted to be bothered, but this guy was ridiculous. The man didn't even know me from a can of paint. He probably doesn't even know which paint brush to use if he had the opportunity. Gorilla mutt probably don't even know how to stroke it right. Okay, I'm a little drunk right now. God don't like ugly, and yes, gorilla mutt is God's child too, so I can't be mean.

He was all up in my face though, asking, *"What yo name is? What yo number is?"*

Can't I just sit here and drink my liquor without being disturbed, please? Gorilla mutt was being very persistent, so I kindly asked him to back away from me. I don't care what he thought of me. I heard him mumble under his breath calling me out my name. I paid him no mind. I just wanted to get over my day. It just felt so bad, and I didn't know where I would begin in explaining to myself that everything was going to be all right.

As I sat there stirring my drink about to take another sip when gorilla mutt returned showing nothing, but teeth.

"This nigga here."

I dropped my head, took a deep breath, turned towards him and smiled. I just wanted him to leave me alone. I crossed one arm over the other and asked him his name. He proceeded to tell me, Gerald Mullens. I laughed to myself. Just like I thought, gorilla mutt. Then, I noticed the brother had on a suit. Hold up! Wait. . .a. . .minute! After work attire, or did he just come out in a suit to catch? Men have caught on that a woman likes a man in a suit. Be yourself. A suit doesn't impress me. Any man can put on a suit and look good.

This with him being in a suit intrigued me enough to ask if he had a job, or if he just came out in a suit to attract attention. I haven't been out in a while to actually know if men do suits in clubs. I've gotten a little bit older now, so I leave the clubbing to the younger generation. I still just wanted to drink alone. As he continued to tell me his life story, I tried to look interested, and remain intrigued. I got lost after he switched topics in

The Precious Jewels Monologue

explaining the kinetics on why we should get together and kick it. I am a classy lady. I don't get together with someone and "kick it."

Gerald was 36. He was a force to be reckoned with, and I didn't want to find out what the force was. He just still came at me wrong though. I did my best to be nice. Gerald finally left, but not before he slid me his number.

I called a cab because I had one too many. I know my limit when it comes to drinking. I made sure that I wasn't being followed on my home. Being out alone is a dangerous thing for a woman these days. But it's not just women. Men have started looking over their shoulders as well. I made it home with no problem and made it safely inside my home that my fiancé left me before he passed. That was his gift to me before the wedding, and he suddenly passed two months prior. We were supposed to have our nuptials April 14th. He died in a head-on collision coming home from a business trip. I got the call 4:15 in the morning. Since that day, I haven't been the same. Gerald called me to see if I made it home. I didn't remember ever giving him my number. He explained to me that someone he knew, knew me and asked for my number. I was still buzzing from the drinks I had earlier, and with him calling me, I wanted to continue to drink. It was nice of him to call and check on me but I had to tell him to tell whomever he got the number from knows not to give out phone numbers without asking first. I am old school. You don't give out numbers without permission.

Since I was safe at home, it didn't bother me as much to talk to him because I didn't have to look at him. He seems intrigued enough with me to want to take me out for drinks, and more conversation.

"Damn! What more could he possibly have to say to me?"

All he wanted was my time. I didn't want his time. I was too busy sulking, and feeling sorry for myself. After a while, agreed to meet with him a few days later for drinks. I had to ask God for forgiveness because of the way I acted with him during the first meeting.

As the day went by, it was time to go meet Gerald at the bar where we both met. I walked in looking to see the same man that I met nights before but didn't see him. I sat at the bar waiting for him to show up, and to my surprise, he was already there.

He walked over to me with that same line he said to me nights earlier. Thinking it was someone else with that same line, I turned to look right into Gerald's eyes. He smiled and I smiled back. He cleaned up really well, or maybe it was the lighting because he looked better than the first night. He had my fiancé's eyes.

CHAPTER 18

DeWayne

I've told bae that I didn't want a relationship. All I wanted from her was sex. But I guess I should have told her upfront about how I wanted things. I played with her heart, and now I'm stuck with dealing with her hurt feelings, and a broken heart. I don't have to deal with her heart; all I need to do is stay away, but the sex is so good! Out of respect for my mother, I was taught not to call any woman out of her name, but bae really needs to be called out her name. I digress and remain silent. She is annoying. Don't ask me how she is annoying to me because I can't tell you.

I only see her once a week. Maybe even once every two weeks and I don't tell her anything. Shorty be giving it up like a pro, and when it's over, I bounce. I give her a kiss on the lips to make it seem like I care, and tell her.

"I'll call you later," I'm sure she knows by now that I'm not talking about later as in, in a few hours.

She seems to always answer when I text. But when I really want to get some from her, I call her. She has it bad not answering her phone. So, I texted again. Bae wanted to see me, and I told her that I was with family. I actually hooked up with

The Precious Jewels Monologue

her later that night. More like early the next morning around 1:30. This woman waits up for me. Sometimes, she leaves the door unlocked, so that I can just come in without ringing the doorbell. This makes me wonder how many other men has she left the door unlocked for.

I'm sure eventually she'll stop dealing with me when she gets tired of my nonsense.

The question would be: *"Would she ever get tired of it?"*

Part of me doesn't want her to get tired of me. In the back of my mind, there is something about her that keeps me coming back. Obviously, there is something about me that keeps her letting me in. I sit here treating her like the gum on the bottom of my shoe. I don't necessarily mean to do that, I just love sex and she gives it to me the way I like it. So, you may be wondering why I haven't scooped her up yet. Simple answer. . .I'm not ready. Yeah, right! It's not that I'm not ready. I'm just not ready with her, and I know that's what she wants. But Hell, I'm 38 years old. What in the hell am I going to do with bae when I constantly want to go out? She keeps me coming back. Maybe she'll be the one who tames me from wanting to go out all the time. I have to think about settling down. I'm not ready to settle down, but she seems to pressure me into doing so.

Naw, bae hasn't put a gun to my head or anything. I just know I need to make a decision before I lose her.

She loves me like no other woman. Bae gives me my space. She doesn't call and she rarely text. When she was texting, it was every other day. I don't know if she was trying to prove a point, or just trying to show affection. She was being straight up with me when I asked her if she was screwing somebody else. Men can't handle truthful answers. I asked her to tell me the truth, but I gave her no choice because in the beginning I told her all I wanted was sex. What I need to do is sit down, and talk to her about my feelings. I don't want her to think I'm weak just because I tell her how I feel. She may take it the wrong way and think I finally want to be with her. Really, I don't know what to do. I want her to understand that I'm not completely ready to commit to anything until I get out from under the one I'm in now.

Yeah, I told bae I was single, but the other truth of the matter is that I'm scared. I'll be a man to admit to being frightened about stepping into another relationship because the last one didn't end so well. Everyone goes through their own way of dealing with a breakup. I started having senseless sex. But when I met bae, things changed. Even though I couldn't bring myself to be with her in a relationship, I just wanted to see how she would take me. I was damaged goods. What made me not want to share my world with her is something that I will have to deal with sooner or later.

I don't even have a reason to why I'm calling her *bae* because she doesn't belong to me. How could I have told her to her face that she was annoying? I know I hurt her feelings.

Her response, *"If I annoy you then why are you dealing with me? If I annoy you, and you can't tell me how I annoy you, then just leave me alone. I say that because you only contact me once a week, and that's by text. You don't even call, so how can I annoy YOU?"*

I'm surprised she didn't kick me out. She took a deep breath, exhaled, climbed on top of me, and gave me the most precious kiss that I ever felt. Was this her game? She now knew how I felt, and yet she still gave me what I wanted. Maybe she didn't want to talk about it anymore because it pierced her too much. Now I have to go home with the thought that I hurt someone special because of an ego. Should I even care? I need to, but I can't because she is not who I want to be with.

CHAPTER 19

JaNee`

I won't sit here and say that it's hard to find a decent man. When I say decent, I mean one without baby mama drama, already been married and those who claim they are single, but already have someone waiting for them at home. I want someone waiting for me at home with a home-cooked meal. If not a cooked meal, take me out for a night on the town. But you know what? Until that time comes, I can do those things myself. It doesn't make sense to sit in the house all day and do nothing that has no substance to it. I won't say there is nothing to do and life is boring. I tell people there is nothing boring, there is always plenty to do. Go for a walk, read a book. . .dance. Not everyone will feel the same way you do.

I have friends, but they have their own lives. The kind of life that looks exciting, but in reality, their life is falling apart. I have no reason to be stressed or depressed. I have a great job, no children and no man. The stories I hear about my friends and their men makes me wonder *"would it be worth it to be in a relationship at all?"*

I want it so bad. Maybe I'm concentrating on the wrong thing. Maybe I should just stay focused on the matter at hand.

Coming home from a hard day's work, and all I want to do is relax. I don't feel like being bothered when it has been a stressful day. That should be the time I'd want to get out to ease my mind. Mother didn't tell me it was going to be this hard. What I wouldn't give to talk to her right now.

I remember the conversations we used to have. When we went out together, people thought we were best friends because we were always laughing. Who says that your mother can't be your best friend? We had boundaries. What she said goes, and I respected that. What's funny is her name. Her parents wanted a boy, and they had already picked out the name. When the doctor told them it would be a girl, they still kept the name. My mother's name was Stanley. It became difficult at one point in my life, as I'm sure it was hard for her. She never changed her name in the honor of her parents. During my school days, anything that had to be signed, she would have to come up to my school to show face that she was a woman and not my father. She stopped explaining her name to people because it started getting old. We laughed about that up until she was on her deathbed.

"Baby don't change a thing on the program about my name. Now it's time for you to tell the story of how I got my name. As a

matter of fact, use my nickname, so they will know that I'm a female."

As mother would have it, I used her nickname, "Sugar Doll." I laid my mother to rest three years ago. I still trip on how I look so much like her. Each morning I look in the mirror, I see her reflection looking back at me. I hope I made her proud.

I shouldn't feel sad because she is with me in spirit, so I'm sure she knows how I'm feeling. . .how lonely I am. Well, maybe not too lonely. I met this man, but I'm thinking that he's not ready to settle down. He even went out of his way to tell me *"You annoy me."* It's his own insecurities that has got him annoyed, and he just doesn't know how to handle a real woman like myself. Besides, I have a full plate, and I'm not trying to scrape anything off that plate to make room for his insecurities that he should have taken care of for himself before he ever tried to step to me. As we all know, within the first 15 seconds of two individuals, the man usually knows whether he wants to sleep with the woman.

I must have really caught his attention because here it is three years later, and he's still not ready to move on to the next level. What would it take to move him just a bit to see how

The Precious Jewels Monologue

much I care for him? Let me rephrase that. . .I love this man. Yes, he knows it, and I'm tired of telling him how I feel. I give him his space, I don't text that much and I absolutely do not call him. Maybe that's what I need to start doing.

The question is: *"Would he answer?"*

I don't have time to sit around waiting on one man to say whether he wants to be with me. Men have a strange way of trying to get a woman's attention.

I don't like it when they come up with lame lines like, *"I feel so right with you."* YOU DON'T KNOW ME FROM A CAN OF PAINT!

Ooooooo I wish my mother was here. I need her so much right now. It's time for me to stop bobbing at the bottom of the barrel for rotten apples. I'm going to switch up the game and start picking blueberries. That's just how men are. Men are like blueberries. They are tart and small. I'm not saying that men are not important, I'm saying that there are some that have small minds. Men can't seem to get beyond the *"second brain."*

Did I mention that I love this man? He is everything that a woman would want and more. But yet, I can't seem to get through to him. His mind seems to be preoccupied with other things. What other things? I don't know because I dared not ask him since the day he told me I annoyed him. I should have put him out that night, but I didn't want to be alone. I just wanted to sleep in his arms. He knows I love him, and at one point, he used that against me when he asked for the truth. I gave him the truth, he got angry but kept coming back. If all he wanted was sex, what would give him the reason to be concerned about who I'm dealing with? Maybe, he just wants me all to himself. All I need to do is ask. It's just that simple. And if he doesn't comply, then there is nothing I can do to change the way he thinks or feels. It would be his loss and three years wasted.

The man is quiet. And you know it has been said that you should be wary of the quiet ones. The quiet ones may have something they are hiding. He may just be the type that doesn't talk. I think I broke through that exterior of a man, but I still won't push him. I don't want him to back away from me. What's so special about this man anyway? He's the one playing these childish games with me. He was the one who was being annoying, but I was so blinded by love that I just couldn't see it. I've had a few associates telling me that I was worried about the wrong thing, that he only cares and that's it; he doesn't love me. How can someone care and not love a person? I always thought in order to care, there is some type of love. . .somewhere. This man should be the least of my worries because I have a full plate. I'm sure when my time comes, God will definitely let me know when He is ready for me to have who He wants in my life. Too much thinking about it would probably cause me to lose touch with reality. But I still love that man. I have to be strong enough to take a step back. . .before he takes it for me.

ABOUT THE AUTHOR

Stacey Barlow, is a resident of Texarkana, TX. The award-winning poet decided to venture into a new realm of writing. Stacey is also a former internet radio personality. . .she plans on traveling the world and spreading her love through the art of poetry.

Stacey has appeared on several BlogTalkRadio shows which includes Virtikal Bistro, Vertikal Café, Poetically Spoken, Cyphers Den and hopes to continue to appear on more shows. She has also made an appearance at The Naked Bean Café in Shreveport, Louisiana 2008. Featured in Poetry and Prose Magazine, and contributes her writing skills to Jennings Wire and Elation Magazine.

www.ingramcontent.com/pod-product-compliance
Lightning Source LLC
Chambersburg PA
CBHW070542300426
44113CB00011B/1766